OTHER EXLEY GIFTBOOKS IN THIS SERIES:
A Feast of After Dinner Jokes   A Round of Golf Jokes
A Spread of over 40s Jokes   A Romp of Naughty Jokes
A Bouquet of Wedding Jokes   A Triumph of over 50s Jokes

Published simultaneously in 1996 by Exley Publications in Great Britain, and
Exley Giftbooks in the USA.

12 11 10 9 8 7 6 5 4 3 2 1

Cartoons © Bill Stott 1996
Copyright © Helen Exley 1996
ISBN 1-85015-776-6
A copy of the CIP data is available from the British Library on request. All rights
reserved. No part of this publication may be reproduced or transmitted in any
form or by any means, electronic or mechanical, including photocopy, recording
or any information storage and retrieval system without permission in writing
from the Publisher.
Series Editor: Helen Exley
Editor: Sonya Dougan
Designed by the Pinpoint Design Company
Typeset by Delta, Watford
Printed and bound in Hungary

Exley Publications Ltd, 16 Chalk Hill, Watford, Herts WD1 4BN, UK.
Exley Giftbooks, 232 Madison Avenue, Suite 1206, New York, NY 10016, USA.

Acknowledgements: The publishers are grateful for permission to reproduce copyright
material. Whilst every effort has been made to trace copyright holders, the publishers would be
pleased to hear from any not here acknowledged. "Hints to the Team by their Captain" by J. M.
Barrie. Extracts from The Wit of Cricket by Ian Brayshaw, reprinted by permission of Scholastic
Ltd. Extracts from The Serious Joke Book by George Coote, reprinted by permission of Herron
Books, Australia. Extract from The Michael Green Book of Coarse Sport by Michael Green,
reprinted by permission of Richard Scott Simon Ltd. Extracts from The Punch Book of Cricket
ed. David Rayvern Allen, reprinted by permission of The Punch Library. Extracts from The
World's Best Cricket Jokes by Ernest Forbes and Cricket Widows by Noel Ford, reprinted by
permission of HarperCollinsPublishers, Australia. Extracts from This Sporting Laugh by Norman
Giller and Great Sporting Fiascos ed. Tony Brett Young, reprinted by permission of Robson
Books Ltd. Extracts from Cricket Capers by Arthur Goldman, published by Afrikaanse Pers
Bockhandel, 1964. Extracts from I Say, I Say, I Say by Brian Johnston, reprinted by permission
of Reed Books. Extracts from The Penguin Dictionary of Jokes ed. Fred Metcalf, reprinted by
permission of Penguin Books UK. Extracts from The 2nd Frank Muir Goes Into by Frank Muir
and Simon Brett, reprinted by permission of Virgin Publishing Ltd. Extract from an interview
with Harold Pinter in the Observer, 5th October, 1980.

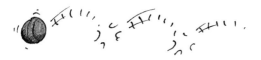

A CENTURY OF

CRICKET

JOKES

CARTOONS BY
BILL STOTT

≡EXLEY
NEW YORK • WATFORD, UK

CAN ANYONE UNDERSTAND THIS GAME!

"WELL, I KNOW IT'S FRUSTRATING, BUT THERE'S NOTHING
IN THE LAWS ABOUT NOT BEING ALLOWED TO BRING
YOUR TEA WITH YOU...."

"Cricket: casting the ball at three straight sticks and defending the same with a fourth."

RUDYARD KIPLING

RULES n, require equivalent of PhD in order to be understood.

P. DUGDALE

•

"Not everyone is able to understand the Englishman's national game. Here is an explanation provided by an English schoolboy: 'You have two sides: one out in the field, one in.

Each man on the side that's in goes out, and when he's out he comes in and the next man goes in until he's out. When they are all out, the side that's been out in the field comes in, and the side that's been in goes out and tries to get those coming in out. Then, when both sides have been in and out twice – including not outs – that's the end of the game.'"

ARTHUR GOLDMAN, from *Cricket Capers*

•

BALL n., imbued with a mind of its own.

P. DUGDALE

"NOT YOUR DAY SON, IS IT?"

An Introduction To Cricket

"I have never got over the shock of seeing my first cricket ball. I simply couldn't believe that there was anything so dangerous loose in what up to then had seemed a safe sort of world."

ROBERT MORLEY

●

"As far as I know, I am the only bowler in the long story of the game who has landed an off-break vertically on the square leg umpire's head. My attempts to bowl fast are even worse, and in the end I gave up after bowling a ball so short that it hit my own foot and I was carried off seriously injured."

from The Michael Green Book of Coarse Sport

●

ALL THIS IS FOLLY...

"To stand upright during so many hours of an extreme heat; to take a violent exercise without any need; to run deliberately a grave danger not less than that which one is obliged to encounter on a field of battle – all this is folly of the most profound. I cannot believe that there is really some pleasure at all in it."

ANATOLE GONJON

●

"In the cricket season I learned there was a safe and far-away place on the field called 'deep' which I always chose. When 'Over' was called I simply went more and more 'deep' until I was sitting on the steps of the pavilion reading the plays of Noel Coward, whom I had got on to after Bulldog Drummond."

JOHN MORTIMER, from *Clinging to the Wreckage*

●

"I do not play cricket, because it requires me to assume such indecent postures."

OSCAR WILDE

The umpire at a village match recognized the batsman as the traffic warden who had given him a parking ticket the day before. The batsman's score was ninety-nine not out when the ball struck him high up on the left thigh.

"Howzat?" said the bowler.

"Out," said the umpire.

The batsman was livid, and as he passed the umpire on the way back to the pavilion he hissed, "You weren't paying attention, I wasn't out."

"Yes, you're right. But I was paying attention!"

●

"Why are the umpires, the only two people on the field who aren't going to get grass stains on their knees, the only ones allowed to wear dark trousers?"

KATHARINE WHITEHORN, from *View From a Column*

●

If at first you don't succeed – blame it on the umpire.

●

"The Devil challenged St Peter to a cricket match. 'Remember,' said St Peter, 'we have all the good cricketers up here.' 'Yes,' said the Devil,' but we've got all the umpires down here.'"

GEORGE COOTE

"HIS <u>BAILS</u>! I SAID – WHIP HIS <u>BAILS</u> OFF!"

"Welcome to Worcester where Barry Richards has just hit one of d'Oliveira's balls clean out of the ground."

BRIAN JOHNSTON

OUCH!

"At Lord's in 1969 Alan Ward bowling very fast from the Pavilion End hits Glen Turner a terrible blow in the box off the fifth ball of his over. Turner collapses in the crease, writhing in pain for about three minutes. He then staggers to his feet looking pale and obviously in great pain.

'Turner has now got up off the ground and, although looking pale and shaken, is obviously going to resume batting. A very brave effort. One ball left!'"

BRIAN JOHNSTON, from *I say, I say, I say*

●

Husband (watching TV): "Joel Garner has come back to bowl with a new ball."

Wife (knitting): "Wonderful what doctors can do these days."

ERNEST FORBES, from *The World's Best Cricket Jokes*

●

WIVES V. CRICKET!

"It's a funny kind of month, October. For the really keen cricket fan it's when you discover that your wife left you in May."

DENIS NORDEN

●

The keen bowler was well into his run up when a row of funeral cars passed the ground. He stopped in his tracks, took off his cap, held it over his heart, and bowed his head. The umpire was impressed.

"You're a man who shows real respect for the deceased," he said.

"It's the least I could do," said the bowler. "After all, she was a good wife to me for thirty years."

●

"Fred's wife snuggled up beside him in bed and whispered: 'Remember the Saturday you proposed to me. My word you were bold then.'

'No way,' said Fred, 'I was caught.'"

GEORGE COOTE

"YOU GOT TEN WICKETS? GOSH – THAT'S NEARLY THE WHOLE TEAM ISN'T IT?"

"IT'S NOT OFTEN YOU SEE UMPIRES PRACTISING."

HINTS TO THE TEAM BY THEIR CAPTAIN

1. Don't practise on opponent's ground before match begins. This can only give them confidence.

2. Each man, when he goes in, to tap the ground with his bat.

3. Should you hit the ball, run at once. Don't stop to cheer.

4. No batsman is allowed to choose his own bowler. You needn't think it.

5. Partridge, when bowling, keep your eye on square-leg.

6. Square-leg, when Partridge is bowling, keep your eye on him.

7. If bowled first ball, pretend that you only came out for the fun of the thing, and then go away and sit by yourself behind the hedge.

J.M. BARRIE

●

The fast bowler was on top form, making even the most fearless of batsmen squirm. He was showing no mercy, taking wicket after wicket. Soon it was the turn of the smallest man on the side to bat. He wore a worried look as he prepared himself at the crease. The sympathetic umpire helpfully asked if the position of the sightscreen was suitable.

"I b-beg your p-pardon," stammered the shaking batsman.

"Would you like the sightscreen moved?" repeated the umpire.

Meekly, the batsman said, looking over at the bowler, "Yes, it would help if it could be moved to a position somewhere between me and that vicious madman there!"

●

"'COURSE IT WON'T MEAN ANYTHING TO YOU YOUNGSTERS – BUT
I REMEMBER WAY BACK IN THE SPRING OF '59...."

BORE n, individual who has been to every Test match series for the past twenty years.

P. DUGDALE

BORED TO DEATH

"It was a hot, sticky afternoon, and the scoring was slow and tedious, when suddenly everyone was wakened by a sharp backfire from a taxi passing the ground.

A voice from the crowd yelled: 'Gawd, the ruddy scorer's shot himself.'"

ARTHUR GOLDMAN, from *Cricket Capers*

●

"Unless you are truly hooked avoid Test matches; they go on too long. I've never forgotten hearing a young man at Lord's saying heartily to his shell-shocked fiancée, 'Don't worry Lavinia, you'll get the hang of it by the fifth day.'"

JILLY COOPER

●

"I don't think I can be expected to take seriously any game which takes less than three days to reach its conclusion."

TOM STOPPARD, playwright-cricket fan, on baseball

A RUDE INTERRUPTION

"A balmy afternoon during a Test match at the Melbourne Cricket Ground was rudely interrupted by a between-overs announcement through the public address system.

'Would Mr J. Smith of Hawthorn please go home,' the voice announced, 'your wife is having her baby and must be taken to hospital.'

Laughter flowed around the ground as the spectators pictured a harassed father-to-be hurrying off home to his wife. Not so, however, because after about half an hour the voice again boomed across the ground, this time with some urgency:

'Repeating our earlier message to Mr J. Smith of Hawthorn... would he please go home immediately, because his wife is in labour and must be taken to hospital straight away.'

Much more mirth from the crowd, this time picturing a man reluctant to leave the cricket – but surely by now bidding farewell to his mates to dash to his vehicle and tear off home. How wrong were 20,000 spectators! Much to their delight the now pleading message was repeated with grim urgency some 20 minutes later. After a further 30 minutes passed there was a bland announcement:

'Would Mr J. Smith of Hawthorn please go to the Mercy Hospital, where his wife has now given birth to a baby son.'"

IAN BRAYSHAW, from *The Wit of Cricket*

●

"The club's best batsman was on the phone to his captain, trying to explain why he couldn't play the next day.

'No, I can't let you off the game,' said the captain, who was made of stern stuff. 'If I did, then I would have to do the same for any other player whose wife dies.'"

GEORGE COOTE

●

A MAN OBSESSED…

"If all the Cricket Widows in the world were laid
end to end, their husbands wouldn't notice until the
end of the cricket season."

NOEL FORD, from Cricket Widows

●

"How do you mean, you had to explain the cricket
match to your wife?"

"She found out I hadn't gone to it."

from The Penguin Dictionary of Jokes

●

His wife was in full flow: "Cricket, cricket, cricket –
that's all you think about. What about us? I bet you
couldn't even tell me what day we were married!"

"Yes I could," replied the husband. "It was the day
Botham scored 147 against the Australians!"

from The Penguin Dictionary of Jokes

●

"SOMEBODY BEEN WASHING THEIR OWN KIT, HAVE THEY?"

COMMENTATOR n, person attempting to make bricks without straw. Inspired waffler.

P. DUGDALE

●

"John Arlott was the master of the microphone who enchanted millions of radio listeners with his poetic view of cricket. When England captain George Mann hit South African left-arm spinner Tufty Mann for six during an Arlott commentary, he described it as 'a case of Mann's inhumanity to Mann.'"

NORMAN GILLER, from "This Sporting Laugh"

●

"So that's 57 runs needed by Hampshire in 11 overs and it doesn't need a calculator to tell us that the run rate is 5.1818 recurring."

NORMAN DEMESQUITA

●

"A wicket could fall in this game, literally at any time."

TREVOR BAILEY

●

"That's a remarkable catch by Yardley specially as the ball quite literally rolled along the ground towards him."

MIKE DENNERS

"... CERTAINLY NOT HAPPY WITH THAT DECISION...."

"His throw went absolutely nowhere near where it was going."

RICHIE BENAUD

Pakistan's record-breaking Hanif Mohammad once annoyed England's fast bowler Freddie Trueman no end with his dead-bat tactics – even against bumpers.

Eventually a fire-breathing Trueman exploded: "If you don't b... well get out of the way, I'll knock you right over," he snorted.

Placidly Hanif replied: "If you mean with your fists, Mr. Trueman, then I'm very frightened. But if you mean with the ball, please bowl me another."

ARTHUR GOLDMAN, from *Cricket Capers*

●

"Augustine Birrell once hit so hard that he smashed the bat I had lent him. Instead of grieving he called out gloriously, 'Fetch me some more bats.'"

J.M. BARRIE

●

"O.K. KELVIN – TEMPT HIM ONTO THE FRONT FOOT – HE LOOKS
WOBBLY THERE – FAILING THAT – KNOCK HIS BLOCK OFF!"

A CRICKETER NEVER FORGETS...

The Middlesex and England cricketer, Denis Compton, once recalled an incident during the New Zealand tour of England in 1949 when the day's play often started at 11.30. Compton was due to bat in the second Test at the Oval, but was held up by traffic at Marble Arch shortly after 11 o'clock.

A motorist in the next car was listening to the match on his car radio when he noticed Compton beside him.

"Shouldn't you be at the Oval?"

"Yes," said Compton. "I'm on my way now."

"But you should be there," said the driver, as he turned up the car radio. "It's an 11 o'clock start."

To the cricketer's horror, he heard the commentator say: "Denis Compton is the next batsman, and he will be coming down the steps any moment now."

from *Great Sporting Fiascos*

"MIDDLE AND LEG HARRY PLEASE... DAMN! I KNEW I FORGOT SOMETHING...!"

"Why are you looking so down-hearted?"

"The doctor says I can't play cricket."

"When did he see you play?"

●

"THE BLOKE DROPPING THINGS? THAT'S OUR WICKET-KEEPER...."

Our wicket-keeper is absolutely hopeless. The only thing he caught all season was whooping cough.

from *The Penguin Dictionary of Jokes*

"Maurice Leyland, the Yorkshire fighter, was getting heckled because of some 'erratic fielding'. One barracker, in particular, was having a 'field day', as he jeered at Leyland's errors.

A roar of delight came from the barracker when poor Leyland dropped a high catch. He yelled: 'Butter fingers. Why, I could have caught it in my mouth!'

Leyland grinned wickedly at the man and said: 'Friend, if I'd a mouth as big as your's, I could have too.'"

ARTHUR GOLDMAN, from *Cricket Capers*

●

The slips had had a bad day, dropping many chances, most of them off the bowling of their captain. Finally they let one ball too many go straight past them. Before they could even straighten from their crouch, the captain carried straight on from his delivery stride, past the batsman, keeper, slips and all, roaring angrily as he thundered past, "It's OK, I'll fetch the damn thing myself!"

●

"During a village match the umpire was heckled by supporters of the home side. After a while he left the field and went and sat down in a deckchair among the noisy spectators. 'What's the idea?' he was asked.

'It appears you get the best view from here,' he replied."

BRIAN JOHNSTON, from *I say, I say, I say*

●

"After a series of bad decisions from the umpire, Ned approached him and said: 'If I called you a stupid old goat who didn't know the first thing about cricket what would you do?'

'I would report you and you would be fined,' said the umpire.

'What if I didn't say it and just thought it?'

'Well, nothing could be done about it.'

'Okay,' said Ned, 'then we'll just leave it at that, then, eh?'"

GEORGE COOTE

●

What happens to a cricketer when his eyesight starts to fail?

He applies to be an umpire.

from *The Penguin Dictionary of Jokes*

IT'S RED AND IT'S ROUND!

Viv Richards once reputedly played and missed against an aspiring fast bowler who promptly made the mistake of giving the master a description of what he had been aiming at. "It's red and it's round," he said.

Richards immediately walked down the wicket and clattered the bowler's next delivery out of the ground and down the road, remarking to his taunter: "Since you know what it looks like, you go and get it."

from *Great Sporting Fiascos*

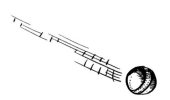

"YOU'VE GOT HIM RATTLED... THAT SIX WENT NOWHERE NEAR AS FAR AS THE OTHERS...."

"I DON'T BELIEVE IT! HE SAYS HE WASN'T OUT, IT'S HIS BALL
AND HE'S GOING HOME!"

DEFINITELY NOT OUT!

"Charles Kortright of Essex, the Demon Bowler, had W.G. Grace caught off his bowling, but Grace refused to go, claiming it had been a bump ball. With his next delivery Kortright flattened two of the doctor's stumps. As Grace departed Kortright called after him 'Why are you going? There's still one stump standing.'"

MIKE SEABROOK

"Did you hear about... the cricketer whose ansaphone message insisted he was not out?"

MARK SLATTERY

CAUGHT OUT?

At a village cricket match they were a man short, so an enthusiastic spectator was enlisted to make up the numbers. He was sent out to long-on, and as the field was on a slope, he was out of sight of the pitch. Apart from throwing the ball in occasionally, he didn't have much to do. After a while a thundering hit was sent in his direction. He caught the ball and ran up the hill, shouting "I caught it, I caught it!"

The batsman was glaring angrily at him.

"You idiot!" he screamed. "They were out 15 minutes ago. We're batting now!"

●

Bowler: "I had three catches dropped today."

Captain: "Yes, but they were dropped by spectators in the stand!"

ERNEST FORBES, from *The World's Best Cricket Jokes*

●

"It's a catch that he'd have caught 99 times out of 1000."

HENRY BLOFELD

●

"WE'VE GOT THEM WORRIED – THEIR CAPTAIN'S DOING THE RAIN

DANCE BEHIND THE PAVILION...."

PUT YOUR BEST TEAM FORWARD!

"Our national cricket team is sensational – no losses, no ties, no runs scored against them."

"How many games have they played?"

"First one's on Sunday."

●

"The cricketer was getting a medical. 'I dunno, Doc,' he said. 'My fielding is very bad lately. I can't bowl like I used to and every time I go in to bat I get a duck.'

'Why don't you try some other sport?' said the doctor.

'I can't,' he said. 'I'm captain of the Australian Eleven.'"

GEORGE COOTE

●

"ACTUALLY, HE'S A DAMN FINE 'KEEPER – WE JUST CAN'T FIND ANY GLOVES TO FIT HIM...."

"Cricketers are reputed to be good lovers. They're fast between the covers and they don't go in without protection."

MARK SLATTERY

●

"I tend to believe that cricket is the greatest thing that God ever created on earth... certainly greater than sex, although sex isn't too bad either. But everyone knows which comes first when it's a question of cricket or sex – all discerning people recognise that. Anyway, don't forget one doesn't have to do two things at the same time. You can either have sex before cricket or after cricket – the fundamental fact is that cricket must be there at the centre of things."

HAROLD PINTER, interviewed in the *Observer*, 5th October, 1980

●

"When I can't play cricket, I subordinate my desire with sex."

ANONYMOUS PUBLIC SCHOOL HEADMASTER

●

"O.K., O.K. – JUST CATCH THE DAMNED THING!"

SHOWING OFF!

"The legendary W.G. Grace was without doubt the peerless batsman of his time and the story has it that modesty was not his problem. He gave ample evidence of this when playing a game in a country town during a tour to Australia.

He faced the first delivery of the game from a rough bushie. To the surprised delight of the bowler and his teammates the champion was clean bowled. But their joy was short-lived. 'never could play the trial ball,' said W.G., as he replaced the bails and took his stance again. The bowler, quite naturally, wasn't taking this lying down and protested strongly, whereupon the bearded Englishman replied, 'Look here, these people have paid to come and see me bat, not you bowl... now let's get on with it.'"

IAN BRAYSHAW, from *The Wit of Cricket*

DOWN, BUT NOT OUT!

"Ned was building up record averages as the club's fast bowler, but he was a little worried when he learned that his father-in-law was to umpire that day's match.

Ned hurled the first ball down at terrific pace and caught the batsman LBW.

'Owzat!' he yelled.

'Not out,' said the umpire.

The second ball came down like a missile, snicked the bat and was caught by the wicket-keeper.

'Owzat!' roared Ned.

'Not out,' said the umpire.

With the wildest fury he could muster, the third ball screamed down the wicket, hit the middle stump and snapped it in half, sending wickets and bails in the air.

'Ruddy well nearly got him that time,' said Ned."

GEORGE COOTE

●

"DON'T BE ALARMED – IT'S JUST THE BOWLERS PRACTISING
APPEALS...."

A Very British Pastime

"Cricket is a game which the British, not being a spiritual people, had to invent in order to have some concept of eternity."

LORD MANCROFT

●

"Cricket is the English version of grand opera. They both seem never-ending, you never know with either of them what's happening at any particular moment and they're both not as good as they used to be."

WILLIAM DAVIS, from *The Punch Book of Cricket*

●

"Sir, I was horrified to learn the other day that there is now a cricket club in Finland. I left England twenty-five years ago to get away from people like yourself. Is nowhere sacred?"

letter to editor of *"The Helsinki Cricketer"*

"SORRY ABOUT THIS, BATSMAN – ANCIENT RIGHT OF WAY...."

STAND BY YOUR MAN...

The fast bowler delivered a ball which flew up and hit the batsman on the head, who had to be taken to hospital for observation. The next day he was introduced to the batsman's wife.

"I'm terribly sorry about what happened to your husband, I feel very bad about it," gushed the bowler.

"Oh, don't worry about it," replied the wife, "I've been wanting to do that myself for years."

●

"Fred's wife rang the cricket club.

'Sorry, he's just walked onto the crease. He is about to bat. Shall I ask him to ring you back?'

'No. I'll hang on,' she said."

GEORGE COOTE

●

Wife, encouragingly: "You take longer to get a duck than you used to, dear."

from *The Punch Book of Cricket*

●

"IT'S THE TEST AND COUNTY CRICKET BOARD – IF YOU THINK
YOU CAN DO ANY BETTER, WOULD YOU LIKE TO PICK THE NEXT
ENGLAND TEAM?"

Through the out-of-form batsman's eyes...

BOWLER: object of ridicule inside the dressing room and reincarnation of Beelzebub when 22 yards away.

BALL: mystery object which finds its way past the edge of your bat but right into the centre of your box.

BOUNDARY: invisible location just beyond wherever you've hit the ball.

Through the eyes of the frustrated bowler...

HELMET: target.

UMPIRE: blind idiot who doesn't know the LBW rules but who can tell to an eighth of an inch where your foot lands.

SLEDGING: a bit of harmless fun between friends which accidentally results in the batsman losing his concentration with either his wicket or his teeth during a purely coincidental spell of hostile fast bowling.

MARK SLATTERY

THE UMPIRE'S WORD IS FINAL...

Dennis Lillee, one of the all-time great Australian fast bowlers, was a fierce competitor, but he always found time for some banter with his favourite umpire, Dickie Bird.

Once after Dickie had turned down his loud LBW appeal, Dennis said: "I think your eyesight's going, Dickie.

"No," replied Dickie, "it's your eyesight that's going. I'm the ice cream seller."

NORMAN GILLER, from *This Sporting Laugh*

●

"I was playing in a match... and as the bowler delivered the ball the umpire ejaculated B-r-r-r- and, after a pause, added:

'I beg your pardon. I meant to say "no-ball," but I dropped my teeth.'"

from a letter to *The Times*

●

"I DON'T LIKE THE LOOK OF THEIR UMPIRE...."

"I've never umpired a cricket match before. Do I have to run after the ball?"

"No, after the match."

ERNEST FORBES, from *The World's Best Cricket Jokes*

"OOH LOOK! A CRICKET MATCH!"

RAIN n, endured in hope by spectators long after all the players have gone home.

P. DUGDALE

RAIN STOPPED PLAY

"Oh God, if there be cricket in heaven, let there also be rain."

SIR ALEC DOUGLAS HOME

"An old witch doctor's son went to England for a holiday and when he came back, his father asked him about English spells and superstitions. 'Oh,' said the boy, 'they have one marvellous ritual. It is called Cricket. A place of sacrifice is prepared with a roller and three ju-ju sticks are dug into the ground at either end. Then eleven men dressed in sacred white robes come out on to the sacred field. And then two more men, also in white, come out, bearing the mighty magic voodoo sticks. Then one of the priests takes a holy ball and throws it at the ju-ju sticks. And as soon as he starts doing that – the rains come pouring down!'"

FRANK MUIR & SIMON BRETT, from *The 2nd Frank Muir Goes Into...*